# THE ASSASSINATION OF JULIUS CAESAR

# THE ASSASSINATION OF JULIUS CAESAR

by
Anthony J. Davies, M.A.
and
Ann B. Davies, M.A.

*Illustrated with drawings, photographs and prints*

*All translations from Greek and Roman writers are by the authors*

FRANKLIN WATTS
London

Franklin Watts Limited,
1, Vere Street,
London, W.1.

SBN 85166 553 5

The publisher wishes to thank the following for their
kind permission to reproduce photographs:
The Trustees of the British Museum, the Radio Times Hulton
Picture Library, Mary Evans Picture Library, The Mansell
Collection, J. Allan Cash.

Jacket by Grace Golden
Maps by Phoebe Posner

Printed in Great Britain by
B.A.S. Printers Limited, Wallop, Hampshire.

# CONTENTS

# ROME

*Showing important buildings erected or begun by 44 B.C.*

Saepta Julia (Voting Hall)

Via Flaminia

Servian Wall

QUIRINAL

VIMINAL

Theatre of Pompey

CAMPUS

Temple of Venus

Portico of Pompey

MARTIUS

Portico of Metellus

T. of Juno

Temple of Venus Genetrix

Forum of Julius Caesar

Curia

Rostra

Basilica Aemilia

market

Fish market

ESQUILINE

Circus Flaminius (possible site)

Ts of Apollo & Bellona

Forum Holitorium

Basilica Julia

Forum Romanum

Regia Via Sacra

Arsenal

Site of Theatre of Marcellus

T. of Jupiter

T. of Castor & Pollux

T. of Vesta

Atrium Vesta

Pons Fabricius

CAPITOL

Insula Tiberina

T. of Aesculapius

Pons Caestius

Temple of Fortuna Virilis

Temple of Cybele

PALATINE HILL

Pons Aemilius

Temple of Vesta

Lupercal

Pons Sublicius (supposed site)

T. of Hercules

Villas until imperial palaces

Circus Maximus

Via Appia

RIVER TIBER

Warehouses

AVENTINE HILL

# INTRODUCTION

On March 15, 44 B.C., Gaius Julius Caesar, the ruler of Rome, walked out of his house surrounded by a crowd of men he believed were his friends. This man had devoted his life to destroying Rome's republican government, and now he was a nearly absolute ruler, king in all but name. He had planned to go to the Roman Senate and make a speech. Shortly afterwards he would join his army for a long campaign abroad.

At the last minute, Caesar almost changed his mind. His wife, not normally a superstitious person, had suffered that night from frightening dreams. She was convinced that some terrible thing would happen if Caesar left the house that morning.

Caesar himself may have been uneasy and, if so, he would have been right, for the crowd of seeming friends was in fact a well-organised conspiracy. They planned in a few minutes to stab Caesar to death.

With smiling faces they had come to his house. They had told him how important it was that he go to the Senate that day. When he hesitated, they reassured him, smiling. They told him to pay no heed to a woman's foolish superstition. The Senate was ready to vote him further honours, they said, and he should not give offence by staying at home.

So he went. Caesar had always been a very lucky man, and his luck almost saved him that day. A well-wisher very nearly managed to warn him of the danger. The Roman-Greek writer Plutarch tells the story:

"Artemidorus, a teacher of Greek philosophy, had become a friend of Brutus, the leader of the conspiracy, and his set, so that he knew most of their plans. He now approached Caesar, holding a document which contained the disclosures that he wanted to make. He saw however that Caesar was taking many documents from petitioners, and passing them all over to his aides, and so he came up close and said, 'Read this at once, Caesar, and read it alone. It is very important, and concerns you personally.'

"Caesar took the document and would have read it, but he was constantly prevented by the mob of people that surrounded him. This was the only paper in his hand as he entered the Senate-chamber....

"Antony was a good friend of Caesar, and a very strong man besides, so Brutus Albinus (another of the conspirators) detained him outside, deliberately engaging him in a long conversation.

"When Caesar entered, the Senate all stood up as a mark of respect, but some of Brutus' party slipped behind the dictator's chair, while others came to meet him. They pretended to be supporting a petition which Tillius Cimber wanted to make, on behalf of a brother who was in exile. Adding their pleas to Cimber's, they escorted Caesar up to his chair.

"After he had sat down, they continued to press him. He continued to refuse, and gradually became angry, until at last Cimber seized the dictator's robe with both hands and pulled it away from his neck. This was the signal for the attack. Casca struck the first blow. His knife made a wound in Caesar's neck, but not a serious one, so that Caesar could still turn round, grasp the knife and hold on.

"The bystanders were all horror-struck. They dared neither run away, help Caesar, nor even make a sound.

"Each assassin now bared his dagger, and they all closed in

on Caesar in a circle, pushing him this way and that, like a wild beast surrounded by hunters. Brutus gave him a blow in the groin. Above all, Caesar had trusted him. Some writers say that Caesar defended himself against all the rest, but when he saw Brutus coming at him with his dagger, he pulled his gown over his head and sank down, either by chance or because his attackers pushed him there, against the statue of his old enemy, the republic's greatest general, Pompey. This statue's pedestal became drenched with blood, for Caesar is said to have received 23 wounds. Many of the conspirators wounded one another as they fought to plant their knives in one body.''

So died one of the most fateful and enigmatic characters the world has ever produced. Great general, politician, poet, statesman, literary critic and mass murderer, Julius Caesar was one of the most remarkable men of all time. By his life and his death he had a crucial influence on the course of history.

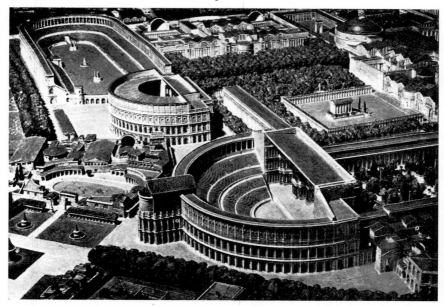

*Reconstruction of Pompey's Theatre Complex (foreground) where the Senate was sitting temporarily when the assassination took place.*

# SENATORIAL OFFICES

CONSUL

PRAETOR

AEDILE

QUAESTOR OR TRIBUNE

# A ROMAN ARISTOCRAT

Gaius Julius Caesar was born, about the year 100 BC, into one of the oldest and proudest families in Rome. Rome was a republic, and had had no king for over four hundred years, but Caesar could boast that some of the kings of Rome had been his ancestors. More recently, however, the family, though very proud and quite rich, had become somewhat obscure. From earliest boyhood Caesar must have had the ambition to make his family as influential as it had once been.

For a Roman aristocrat, family pride was almost everything. When the last king was deposed, in 509 BC, a republic was established where the king's office was divided between two men, elected every year. These officials were called Consuls, and they were supposed to act as a check on each other, so that neither could take over absolute power. To be elected Consul was every rich Roman's dream. The Consuls were supported and advised by a Senate of the richest and most aristocratic landowners (Rome was originally a farming community) and they were responsible both to the Senate, and to the rest of the citizen body, who could come together in a mass meeting to vote, and to make laws. The politically ambitious Roman would enter the Senate and try to be elected, by the people, to a series of offices, of which the Consulship was the last and greatest.

In practice, almost all of the Consuls were drawn from the small, privileged landowning class that made up the Senate. By Caesar's youth, there were only about 300 senators. They all knew each other very well and formed an exclusive, self-perpetuating club which effectively governed the country. To win elections, a man needed

11

allies, and he usually found these among the other great families, who would band together to try to elect as many of their members as they could to public office.

In the centuries before Caesar, this system worked very smoothly. While the people could theoretically make laws and did elect the magistrates, all the experience and all the initiative lay with the Senate. An ambitious Roman could work quietly within the club, advancing his career and giving no-one much trouble, secure in the knowledge that, with the help of his friends, he could be fairly sure of winning the high offices that he craved. Once he had been Consul, he would have gained the "dignity"—an important word in understanding the Roman mind—he needed, and could then retire. He would have upheld the honour of his family and would be respected by all. In the quietest period of the republic, this was the finest thing which life offered. "Quiet"; "respect"; "peace with dignity" : these are some of the phrases which Romans of this period used to describe their ambitions.

This is what Caesar could have expected of his career if times had not changed. Of course, he would have needed to work harder than the average young man in his position, because his family had somewhat fallen into the background of Roman political power, but he still had strong friends and good family connections. All things considered, his future was bright and he could reasonably expect to win as many political offices as he was capable of reaching—and Caesar was an extremely capable man.

Instead of quietly following this path, rising in the political structure, and perhaps with luck even gaining its highest office, Caesar's career was changed by what was happening in the world around him. The final result was that he gained greater power than Rome had ever known, and became a figure half-clouded in legend, who has fascinated the world ever since.

What had happened was that the small, self-contained city-state of Rome had conquered more territory than it knew how to govern

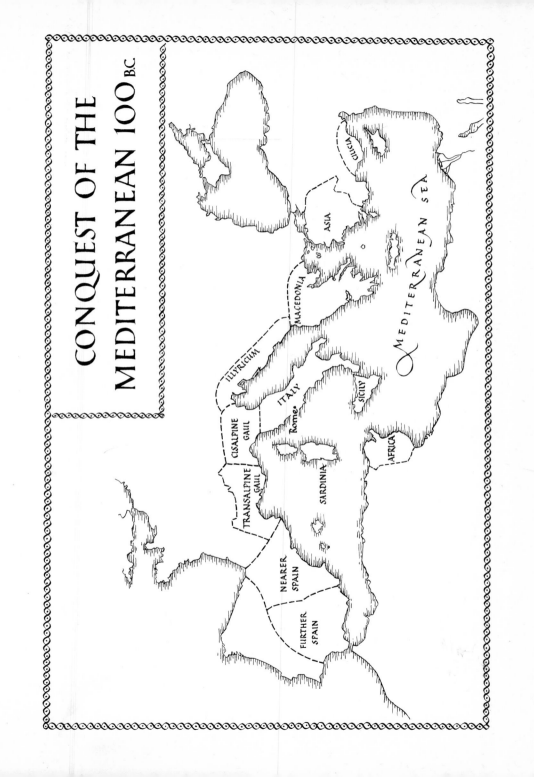

# CONQUEST OF THE MEDITERRANEAN 100 B.C.

CILICIA

ASIA

MACEDONIA

ILLYRICUM

MEDITERRANEAN SEA

CISALPINE GAUL

ITALY

Rome

SICILY

TRANSALPINE GAUL

SARDINIA

AFRICA

NEARER SPAIN

FURTHER SPAIN

effectively. The senatorial club had been adequate to govern Rome when it remained small, but with Rome's conquest of the whole Mediterranean, the Senate was too conservative and inflexible to take on the added difficulties of governing this large area. The stresses that resulted from the Senate's inability to handle the ensuing multitude of problems eventually brought down the republic. Rome, during this period, was rocked by the activities of a series of power-hungry men, of whom Caesar was the last and most successful.

Much of Rome's trouble at this time was economic. There had grown up in Rome a large group of citizens who were too poor to support themselves. Many of these poor people were former farmers who had lost their land. It was a peculiarity of the Roman system that the only men liable for conscription into the army were those who had a certain amount of money—enough, in fact, to pay for their own kit. When Rome's interests extended no farther than Italy, it was no hardship for such a man, who was likely to be a small farmer, to be conscripted for a summer campaign, fight a few battles and then return home in time for the harvest. However, when Rome began to fight wars farther away, in Greece, Asia, or Spain, a man's military service would often keep him away from home for several years. His wife would do her best to run the farm in his absence, but there was every chance that when he came home he would find his farm in ruins, perhaps mortgaged or sold to a creditor. With his livelihood gone, the farmer would drift to Rome with his family, to swell the ranks of the ever-growing urban poor.

Thus the farmlands were being emptied of people, as they fell into the hands of the rich, while the population of Rome grew and grew. This created a dangerous situation. Unscrupulous politicians could make use of a dissatisfied group of this kind.

Again, many of the unemployed poor in Rome would have been glad to serve in the army as a way of making a living, but were unable to do so, because they were too poor to qualify for enlistment. If the army had been able to take these men, in place of the small farmers

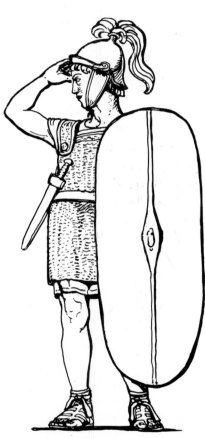

*Uniform of Roman legionary about the time of Caesar.*

*Top of legionary standard*

who did not want to serve, much of the state's economic problem could have been solved. Instead, for a long time nothing was done. It was only in 107BC that the politician-general Marius began to recruit very poor men for the army, without the sanction of the Senate, and in response to the urgencies of a war in Africa. But this measure set a far-reaching precedent and, while it solved the problem of the draft and went a long way towards relieving the poor farmers of Italy, it had an unfortunate side-effect. The men thus recruited were no longer citizen-militia, territorials or reservists called up at need and then stood down when the campaign was over. They tended to become long-term professional soldiers, who had few ties with civilian life, and whose loyalty came to be centred chiefly on their commander, rather than in the government at Rome. Such troops proved very easy to lead into civil war.

The Senate was unwilling to pay attention to these and other problems. The people were eager to listen to anyone who showed concern for their difficulties. Many politicians from the senatorial class saw the chance of working through the people in their distress, and taking advantage of the popular assembly's new militancy to gain influence for themselves in the Senate.

Here was the crucial danger. In the Roman system, politicians were often given command of armies, as well as civilian jobs. A man with a large popular following might be tempted to use his army against the Senate. This in fact happened many times during Caesar's lifetime. While Caesar was growing up, Rome was greatly disturbed by the activities of these politician-generals. The most famous were Marius and Sulla.

# CAESAR'S EARLY LIFE

The young Caesar's adolescence was very much what one would expect from someone with his family background. One factor, however, complicated the course of his life and ultimately gave him the opportunity to prove his ability in a way that might otherwise never have come to him.

Caesar's aunt Julia was the wife of Marius, who had served as Consul seven times, and had often availed himself of the support of the devoted army that he had, as general, personally recruited. Marius was a great general who came from the minor aristocracy. He was anti-Senatorial in his views and was a politician who had succeeded by the novel method of working directly through the people. He had a very strong enemy in Sulla, who was a leader of the conservative group, a faction often known as the *Optimates*, or "Party of the Best Men". These two great generals in turn dominated Rome in the 80's BC. First Marius was in control while Sulla and his army campaigned in the East. Then, following Marius' death in 86, Sulla returned to Rome at the head of his army to deal with Cinna, one of Marius' lieutenants, who was then in power. In 82 a very bloody civil war ensued which left Sulla the complete master of Rome. He became a dictator and proceeded to rid Rome of the remainder of his opponents, a group known as the *Populares*, or "Party of the People". His regime was marked by such cruelty that it was never forgotten.

This is where we find Julius Caesar after Sulla's counter-revolution. His connection through his aunt with Marius, as well as his own marriage to a daughter of one of Marius' friends, put him in the most

17

unfortunate position of being aligned with the *Populares*, although at this point Caesar had not yet done anything actively political. All this brought him to the dictator's attention. Sulla must have seen promise in the young man, for he tried to win him over to his side. Caesar showed great courage in steadfastly opposing the dictator's demand that he divorce his wife, and marry a lady acceptable to the dictator. Sulla made a similar request of a man named Pompey, who later became Caesar's great enemy. Pompey complied.

Fearing for his life, Caesar fled Rome, only to be brought back to face Sulla. By the intercession of friends his life was spared. The Roman historian Suetonius tells of Sulla's insight into the young man's character, when he gave his hesitant pardon, and said to Caesar's friends: "All right, have your way and take him. But just realise that this man that you so much want to save will be the death of the aristocracy, which we have all been defending. There are many Mariuses in Caesar."

Even though he had been pardoned by Sulla, Caesar must have felt that he would be safer away from Rome. He went off with Marcus Thermus, governor of Asia and a friend of Sulla, and served in the army with great distinction. In this manner his career was launched.

On learning of Sulla's death in 78, Caesar immediately returned to Rome. His military apprenticeship behind him, he could now turn his attention to making his name known by the time-honoured way of prosecuting people for corruption. Between 78 and 75 he brought charges against two Sullan officials. Although he failed to convict them, he made a very good impression as a speaker.

(left) Sulla, and (right) gold coin issued by him.

19

His next move was to the island of Rhodes, where he studied oratory under the great Greek professor Apollonius Molo. At this time something happened that well illustrates Caesar's character. On his way to Rhodes he was captured by pirates, who were at that time a deadly menace to all travellers. What happened next is worth recounting at length. Plutarch tells the story.

"When the pirates first demanded that he pay 20 talents [a large sum of money] by way of ransom, he laughed, saying

*(left) Reconstruction of Roman trireme and (above) Roman galley as depicted on a coin.*

that they did not know whom they had captured, and offering to give them fifty. Then, when he had sent most of his friends around the various cities to raise the money, he was left among the pirates—some of the most murderous in the world—with only one friend and two servants. Even so, he was not the least afraid, and went so far, when he wanted to sleep, as to send and tell them to be quiet.

Caesar spent thirty-eight days among the pirates, treating them less as jailers than as royal bodyguards, and cheerfully sharing in all their amusements and exercises. To pass the time he wrote numerous poems and speeches, which he insisted on reading to his captors. If they were not sufficiently appreciative, he would abuse them for ignorant barbarians, and often laughingly declared that one day he would crucify them all. The pirates were highly entertained, putting his free way of talking down to a kind of childish simplicity.

Then the ransom came from the nearby city of Miletus. Caesar paid it and was freed, but immediately manned ships and put out from Miletus' harbour in pursuit of the pirates. He caught them still anchored off their island base, and captured most of them.

Having captured both men and money, he threw them into jail at Pergamon, the seat of the governor of Asia. The governor, however, hoped for a ransom himself, and refused to punish them immediately. Caesar simply ignored him, took the robbers out of jail and crucified them all, as he had often threatened to do, while he was at their mercy and they thought he was joking."

Suetonius adds that Caesar was humane enough to cut the pirates' throats before crucifying them.

After Caesar's return to Rome in 73, he spent the next few years in holding a number of the minor offices every young Roman had to fill, before he was eligible to stand for the important positions that

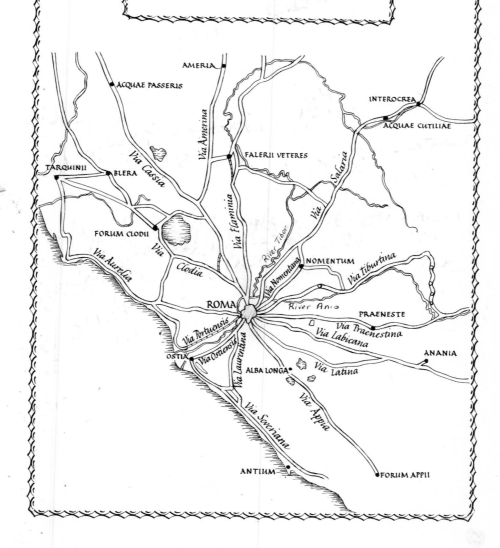

# ROMAN ROADS

*(Map labels:)*

AMERIA
ACQUAE PASSERIS
INTEROCREA
ACQUAE CUTILIAE
Via Amerina
FALERII VETERES
Via Cassia
TARQUINII
BLERA
Via Salaria
Via Flaminia
FORUM CLODII
Via Aurelia
Via Clodia
River Tiber
NOMENTUM
Via Tiburtina
Via Nomentana
ROMA
River Anio
PRAENESTE
Via Portuensis
Via Praenestina
Via Labicana
ANANIA
OSTIA
Via Ostiensis
Via Laurentina
ALBA LONGA
Via Latina
Via Appia
Via Severiana
ANTIUM
FORUM APPII

he really wanted. There was a variety of these minor jobs. The young politician could be a member of a board that looked after the coining of money. He could also be a minor functionary in the penal system, or he could take a very short military commission. Julius Caesar was elected to a position in the army—something comparable in importance to a modern lieutenant's commission—and he carried this election by a very great majority. Already he was building up that popularity with the ordinary voter which was to be one of his great assets all his life.

This period of minor offices lasted until 70, when Caesar stood for the first in the ladder of important elections, which might eventually lead him to the head of the state. This was the office of Quaestor. The Quaestor was a kind of financial official, who had a position of great trust, either in the public treasury at Rome, or on the staff of a provincial governor. By being elected Quaestor, Caesar was also admitted to the Senate. As it turned out, he was posted to the staff of the governor of Spain. Here he seems to have done well. There is a story, quoted by Suetonius and possibly true, that when Caesar was in the town of Gades in Spain (modern Cadiz) he noticed a statue of Alexander the Great. On seeing it he sighed, because Alexander, when in his thirties, had conquered half the known world, while he himself had not yet done anything remarkable.

*(left) Engraving of Caesar before Alexander's Statue, and (above) head of Alexander.*

# THE JULIAN FAMILY TREE

Venus
|
*Many generations of*
*mythical heroes*
|
Romulus
*first King of Rome*
|
Ancus Marcius
*King of Rome*
|
Julian Gens

Marius=Julia    Gaius Julius Caesar=Aurelia

Cornelia(1)=JULIUS CAESAR = Pompeia(2) = Calpurnia(3)
*daughter of Cinna*    *grand-daughter*    *daughter of Piso*
|    *of Sulla*
Julia=Pompey

*The claim of the*
*Julian family to be*
*descended from the*
*Kings of Rome.*

Another interesting event during Caesar's Quaestorship was the death of his aunt Julia. As was the custom, Caesar made a public speech in her memory. His speech was unusual, however, in that he mainly described how she was descended from the family of the ancient kings of Rome. It may be that even as a young man, Julius Caesar had ideas of reviving the kingship, which had been abolished at Rome for well over four hundred years.

# THE SIXTIES

When Caesar returned from Spain in 68 he knew that, if all went well, only nine years of political activity stood between him and the Consulship, the highest regular office in the land. This was the time for a far-seeing man to map his strategy for getting to the top, and Caesar chose the way of intrigue.

He needed help, and the logical thing was to attach himself to someone with greater influence, who could make use of his talents.

At this time two over-mighty politicians, Gnaeus Pompeius Magnus and Marcus Licinius Crassus, had each achieved great military reputations, and with them an eminence which allowed them to threaten the normal workings of the constitution. Pompeius— Pompey as he is usually known—was a brilliant general who was mostly interested in getting himself appointed to command in future wars. Crassus was a very wealthy man who enjoyed using his money to manipulate affairs—chiefly, it seems, for the pleasure that he got out of wire-pulling. Pompey and Crassus hated each other, but Caesar, considerably their junior in age and status, was tactful enough to be able to work for both of them in different ways, always advancing his own interests.

In fact, one of Caesar's great assets was that, when he chose, he could be utterly charming, as well as tactful. He needed all his charm to bring Pompey and Crassus together. He was also somewhat of a dandy, and early in his career this disarmed many of his opponents, who could not bring themselves to take him seriously.

Pompey and Crassus were much too egotistical to work closely

*Pompey.*

together, but really they had many interests in common. In particular, they were opposed by all the conservative elements in Roman society, men who feared dictatorship if too much power collected in the hands of one individual. Caesar hoped to be someone like Pompey and Crassus one day, so it is natural that he should have supported their aims. In fact he hoped eventually to replace them, but first he must rise on their shoulders. So he spent the years 68-59 BC working for these two men, and generally against the old-fashioned constitutionalists, but taking every chance to win friends, and build up his own prestige.

In 67 Rome was faced with a serious war against the pirates who were terrorising the Eastern Mediterranean. These raiders had almost brought commerce to a stop, and the whole coast of Italy was at their mercy. A series of republican commanders had done little to suppress them, and Pompey was the logical man to send. In order to be effective though, he would have to have a command of unusually wide scope, and this was something which most conservatives quite rightly feared. Caesar was the only junior Senator to speak in favour of Pompey being given this command. Pompey went East and subdued the pirates in three months.

Again in 66 a man like Pompey was needed in the East, this time to fight King Mithridates, who had been challenging Rome's control of Asia Minor for several years. This was an issue which touched Crassus, who was, above all else, a businessman. He had large interests in Asia and he stood behind a whole class of businessmen who were losing money as long as Mithridates was loose. Mithridates was even murdering Roman merchants whenever he could. So the measure to give Pompey supreme command in the East (a dangerous con-stitutional novelty to the Roman republic) easily passed over the objections of the conservatives. Again, Caesar spoke in support of it.

These and other actions made it clear what kind of path Caesar was following. But, not being content to remain the tool of Pompey and Crassus, he worked with great skill on building up an independent

*Coin of Mithridates the Great.*

*Gold coins of the Pompey family.*

position. In 65 Caesar was one of the board of Aediles, elected officials who looked after the day-to-day management of the city of Rome. These men regulated the markets, made sure the streets were kept clean, and organised gladiatorial games. These shows, a poor Roman's chief source of entertainment, were paid for out of public funds, but an ambitious Aedile would often spend a lot of his own money on them, hoping that the people would remember his generosity when he was standing for future offices. Caesar was no exception, but he was clever enough to spend other people's money instead of his own. He and a fellow-Aedile, Marcus Calpurnius Bibulus, had to put on some games together. Bibulus was a very conservative aristocrat, and a bitter rival of Caesar. Even so, it turned out that most of the money for the show came from Bibulus, and Caesar took most of the credit. Caesar had a great talent for doing things like that. Bibulus was unlucky enough to be the same age as Caesar, and under the Roman system the two men held office in the same years throughout their lives. Bibulus always seemed to come off second best.

The late 60's were a time of increasing unrest at Rome. Rumours abounded of conspiracies against the state. Crassus' name keeps turning up as a backer of possible revolutionaries, and Caesar, known to have been Crassus' agent from time to time, was also under suspicion. There are stories about one such plot in 65, directed against the Consuls of that year. At a signal from Caesar they were to be slain by a group headed by their disappointed rivals, and in the confusion Crassus and Caesar were to put themselves in charge of affairs. If there was such a plot, it never came to anything, and we have no way of knowing if Caesar was really implicated. The ancient sources put Crassus' name in the plot with much more certainty than Caesar's, and it is quite likely that the accusation of Caesar comes from the propaganda of his conservative enemies. What is clear, however, is that he was very friendly with men who were suspected of wanting revolution. Some of Crassus' other allies may have been involved, but Caesar himself was probably waiting for bigger things.

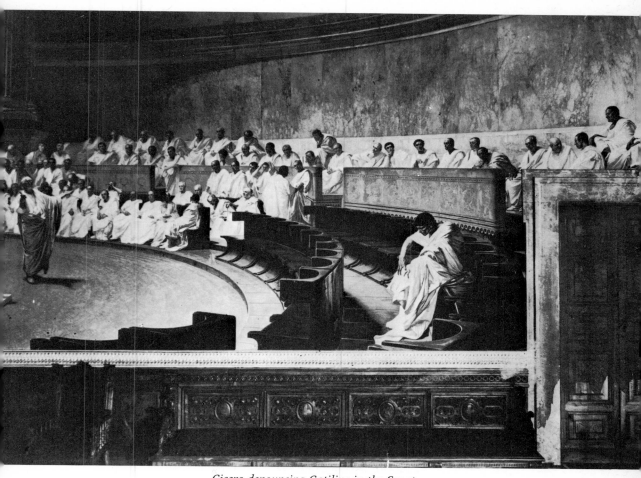

*Cicero denouncing Catiline in the Senate.*

In 63 came a more serious conspiracy. Lucius Sergius Catilina, a violent aristocratic spendthrift who was possibly mixed up in the affair of 65, had stood for the Consulship in 63. He was not elected and, in desperation, being very short of money, he organised a large-scale plot involving murder of most of the Senate, a popular uprising and the cancellation of all debts. This man, known to us as Catiline, had in his day been a *protegé* of Crassus, but it is not likely that Crassus was much involved in this plot. In fact, he was warned by an anonymous letter of what was to happen; he notified the Consul Cicero, and the latter took energetic measures to arrest all the conspirators in Rome. This whole conspiracy was remembered by the Romans as perhaps a more serious matter than it actually was; it was a plot as celebrated in Rome as the Gunpowder Plot of Guy Fawkes has always been in Britain. Again, rumour connected Caesar with the conspiracy. A debate took place in the Senate over what to do with the arrested plotters, and by a skilful speech Caesar almost persuaded the Senate to spare their lives. In this he was successfully opposed by Marcus Porcius Cato, a very able supporter of the constitution, who declared that Caesar was working to make himself dictator. Cato's speech was so effective, we are told, that Caesar was almost lynched.

Caesar was never afraid to go into debt, either to help a friend or to buy an election. In 63 he was elected Chief Priest—a job with considerable political importance—and to secure this he spent almost everything that he had, plus much more that he had borrowed, in bribing the voters. In fact, his financial state was so desperate that he is said to have told his mother, on the morning of the election, that he was going down to the polls and, if not elected, he would never come home again.

Again in 61 he was preparing to set off for a year as the Governor of Spain. The journey was, of course, at government expense, but he was still so much in debt that his creditors tried to prevent him by force from leaving Rome. They seized his baggage and would not release it until Crassus paid his debts.

*Caesar in priestly robes.* ▷

Caesar's brief spell in Spain was his first experience of an independent military command. Perhaps rather to his surprise, he found that he had a real talent for generalship, and it may have been at this time that he decided to pursue his career in the army. When he returned to Italy after a successful year, Caesar was ready to stand for election to the Consulship. To succeed in the face of the hatred which he had already caused among many conservatives, he needed money and powerful friends more than ever. Crassus was still available, and Pompey could also be of help. The latter was now back after a triumphant campaign against King Mithridates, but he too was hated by many conservatives, and he happened to be so incompetent at political manoeuvering that, in spite of his great prestige, he needed help in order to maintain his position.

So Pompey, Crassus and Caesar drew together in an alliance. Caesar was the junior partner, and it is a tribute to his powers of diplomacy that Pompey and Crassus ever agreed to co-operate at all. The three men arranged to work for Caesar's election as Consul in 59. He would be eligible for a big military command on leaving office, and as Consul could look after the interests of the other two.

Nothing shows Caesar's talents more clearly than the way in which he managed the election. Suetonius tells the story.

"There were two other candidates for the Consulship, Lucius Lucceius and Marcus Bibulus. Caesar joined forces with Lucceius, with the understanding that Lucceius, who had less popularity and more money, would promise bribes to the voters in both their names, but out of his own pocket. When the conservatives heard this, they were afraid that Caesar would stop at nothing, if elected to the highest office with a sympathetic colleague. So they authorised Bibulus to promise the same amount, and even Cato did not deny that this bribery was for the good of the state. So Caesar was elected Consul with Bibulus."

It is not difficult to guess how Lucceius felt towards Caesar after the election.

# CAESAR'S CONSULSHIP

The fateful year of Julius Caesar's Consulship shows him at his best and at his worst. When he took office, the conservatives shuddered, and expected all sorts of revolutionary measures. Caesar, however, began moderately. He announced that in everything he did he would act with scrupulous regard for the law, and he emphasised this by ostentatiously deferring at times to his colleague (and enemy) Bibulus.

In fact Caesar, who always believed in making all the friends that he could, and not making unnecessary enemies, was prepared to work through the Senate. When the time came for him to offer a measure to grant land to Pompey's veterans, he took this proposal to the Senate. There he read it through, politely requested their support, and asked for suggestions. The conservatives in the Senate were horrified, because the bill was modest, sensible and well-drafted. They could think of no comments short of outright rejection, and that is what Cato very unwisely persuaded them to do. Loudly protesting that the Senate was forcing him to extreme measures, Caesar walked out, and immediately laid his proposal before the assembly of the people, who had as much right as the Senate to pass such legislation. Bibulus attempted to interfere, but Caesar brushed him aside, and, to make doubly certain of getting the result he wanted, brought in some of Pompey's veterans to the voting place. The measure was quickly passed.

From now on, Caesar was openly at odds with the traditionalist

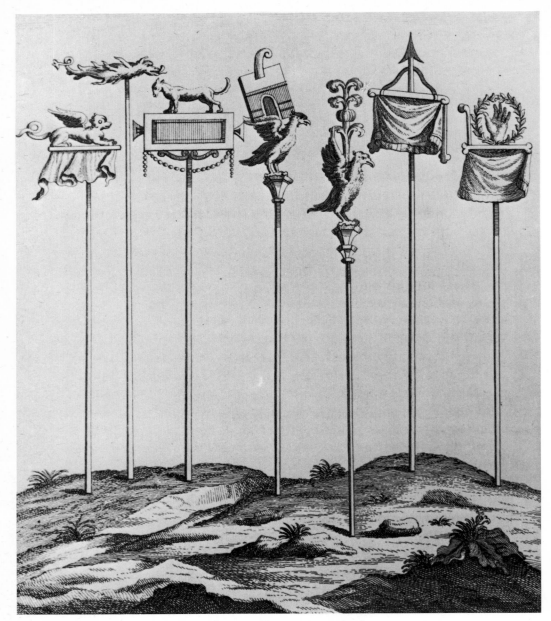

*A selection of legionary standards.*

faction in the Senate, but these men had an important weapon left to them, the other Consul Bibulus.

Roman life was bound up to a great extent with religious ceremonial, some of it very primitive superstition. In particular, no business of any kind could legally be conducted, if the omens were unfavourable. Bibulus now began a systematic campaign of religious obstruction to everything that Caesar did. At an early stage in these proceedings, he was driven out of the forum by the violence of Caesar's supporters—in itself quite illegal—but he retired home and from there proceeded to veto every action of Caesar's. This he did by announcing every day that he was watching the sky for unfavourable omens, such as certain birds or a flash of lightning. This by itself should have been enough to stop all business, but Caesar took absolutely no notice.

In fact Bibulus hardly appeared out of doors for the rest of the year, and Caesar seemed to be the only Consul in Rome. Suetonius says that many people made jokes about this, sealing up bogus documents, which should have been marked "Done in the Consulship of Caesar and Bibulus", with the words "Done in the Consulship of Julius and Caesar". However, in so disregarding his colleague, Caesar had made a fateful decision. His action was blatantly illegal, and he knew that one day he might be prosecuted for it. Yet under the Roman system no public official could be prosecuted *while still in office*. So from this time on, Caesar knew that if he were ever a private citizen, even if only for one day, he would certainly be prosecuted, and his political career—and possibly his life—would be at an end. This problem hung over him for the next ten years and, when he finally had to face a choice between laying down public office and starting a civil war, he had very little hesitation in choosing the latter course.

The rest of Julius Caesar's actions as Consul show the same strange mixture of responsible, far-sighted statesman and unscrupulous, violent politician. The measure about Pompey's veterans, however

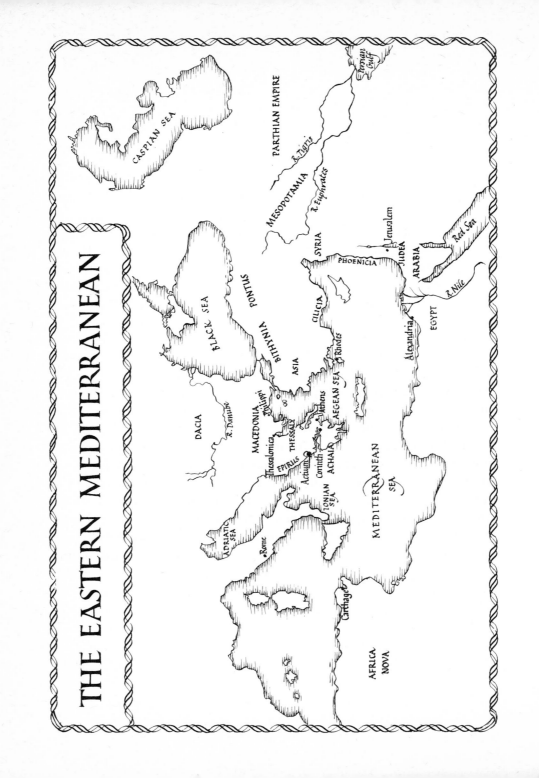

# THE EASTERN MEDITERRANEAN

CASPIAN SEA

PARTHIAN EMPIRE

Persian Gulf

R. Tigris

MESOPOTAMIA

R. Euphrates

SYRIA

• Jerusalem

Red Sea

JUDEA

PHOENICIA

ARABIA

BLACK SEA

PONTUS

CILICIA

R. Nile

BITHYNIA

ASIA

Rhodes

Alexandria

EGYPT

AEGEAN SEA

DACIA

R. Danube

MACEDONIA

Philippi

Athens

Thessalonica

THESSALY

EPIRUS

Corinth

ACHAIA

Actium

IONIAN SEA

MEDITERRANEAN SEA

ADRIATIC SEA

• Rome

• Carthage

AFRICA NOVA

illegally carried through, was sensible and necessary, as was the recognition which he gained from the people of the many arrangements that Pompey had made for the government of the East, at the end of the war with Mithridates. There was little justification, however, for the way in which Caesar paid off his debt to Crassus. This man, as we have seen, was the champion of much of Rome's commercial interests. Many of Crassus' friends were involved in collecting taxes in the East of the Roman Empire. They worked under a curiously Roman system of extreme private enterprise. Instead of the taxes being collected directly by the government, contracts for this purpose were given out under tender to private tax-collecting companies, who made what money they could by shamelessly extorting money from the wretched provincials. This year Crassus' friends wanted a large reduction in the amount of money which they would have to pay into the Roman treasury, since they had bid too high. Caesar as Consul was able to arrange this and, when Cato tried to object, Caesar had him temporarily thrown into prison.

On two occasions Caesar was on the point of having Cato jailed. Such arbitrary action, though unusual, was well within a Consul's power. The first time he wanted to punish him for obstruction in the Senate, but when Cato was being led away, the whole Senate followed him, and Caesar, seeing how much feeling was against him, relented. Another time, Cato was being dragged away after trying to speak to the people against a proposal of Caesar's. Then too, Caesar saw that what was happening did not please his audience, and gave a hint, so Plutarch says, to a Tribune of the People (*see note, page* 95) to veto Cato's arrest. He finally had Cato rendered harmless by sending him on an honourable, but quite useless mission abroad. Caesar's treatment of Cato at this time shows a very important aspect of his character; his ability to understand when he had made a mistake and to correct himself.

For himself, Caesar needed a military command. When Consuls left office, they were automatically given a prestigious and respon-

sible job, usually the government of a province, with command of an army. Such a command would have given Caesar protection from his enemies, who now badly wanted to prosecute him. He would also have an opportunity to win fame (and perhaps money) as a general, and to gain control of a body of soldiers who might help him, if ever he thought of civil war.

For this reason it was particularly frustrating for him to find, when he became Consul, that the Senate had voted that after his year of office he would not take a regular province, but would instead be given charge of "The Woods and Cattle-Drifts of Italy". Caesar had no intention of wasting time as a kind of forestry-commissioner, so he enlisted the help of a sympathetic Tribune of the People named Vatinius to get him the kind of command that he wanted. Luck was on his side. The man to whom the Senate had voted the command in Gaul and Illyricum—an area then extending along the coasts of what are now Southern France and Yugoslavia—happened to die. Vatinius proposed to the people that Caesar should be given this command. The people enthusiastically agreed, and the Senate, who could not override such a vote, found that Caesar was after all to have command of an army.

His future was thus safe for the time being. The command was to last for five years, and was in fact later renewed to run until 49 BC. At the end of his command Caesar might hope to stand for a second Consulship and, if successful, begin a second round of public offices which would increase his prestige and, above all, keep him out of the law courts. There were serious constitutional problems ahead, but with his two powerful allies, the support of the people, and the following of subordinate politicians that he was collecting in his own right, Caesar could be quite confident.

◁ Cato.

# ITALY

## SHOWING ROME AND THE RUBICON

ALPS

CISALPINE GAUL

R. Po

Mantua

Placentia

R. Rubicon

Luca

Ariminum

Arretium

R. Tiber

CORSICA

ADRIATIC SEA

ROME

Corfinium

Formiae

Capua

SARDINIA

Brundisium

Tarentum

SICILY

# GAUL

When Caesar went to command the army in Gaul, this must have given general satisfaction. The Gallic tribes who owed no allegiance to Rome were rough and warlike and, if he were to fight them, he might expect to make a name for himself as a commander. Conversely, his enemies hoped that the Gauls would be too much for Caesar; in five years he might be killed, or at least severely discredited. In this expectation they turned out to be very wrong.

To the Romans, "Gaul" extended far into what we call Italy (*see map opposite*). In 58 BC Roman-held Gaul included the Italian peninsula north of the River Po in northern Italy, as well as a small strip of land between Italy and Spain. This region, one of the first to be conquered by Rome outside Italy proper, the Romans often called "The Province" (Latin *Provincia*), and it is still known as Provence. North of this coastal strip were numerous Gallic tribes, fierce, independent and mostly suspicious of Rome. A few of them, however, notably the Aedui and the Sequani, had treaty-relations with Rome and, if Caesar needed an excuse for interfering north of Roman Gaul, it would be there, if one of these friendly states asked for his protection.

An opportunity soon came. As early as 60 BC the Helvetii, a tribe who lived in what is modern Switzerland, decided to migrate to better lands in Western Gaul. They spent two years getting ready, and by 58 they were on the move. To cross the mountains they could either take a route through Roman Gaul, or they could move

45

*Ariovistus is defeated by Caesar*

north-west through the territory of the Sequani. Early in 58 they asked Caesar's permission to move through his province. Looking for a fight, he refused. They then applied to the Sequani, who agreed. However, the Sequani were friends of Rome and, when they complained to Caesar that the Helvetii were looting and doing damage to their country, he had his pretext for marching north. After a few short and bloody battles, the Helvetii were compelled to go home, but once Caesar's army was in free Gaul, it stayed.

One intervention led to another. Caesar and his army were a new factor in the politics of Gaul, and it was only to be expected that one faction would call him in against its enemies. Immediately after the defeat of the Helvetii, a number of tribes, including Rome's friends the Aedui, called on Caesar to help them against the German king Ariovistus, who was pushing across the Rhine into Gaul. This was slightly awkward for Caesar, as Ariovistus himself had only recently been recognised as a friend and ally of Rome—we do not quite know why. Caesar solved this problem by meeting with Ariovistus and asking him to cease from interfering with Rome's friends in Gaul. As was probably expected, the king lost his temper, made a number of insulting remarks to Caesar, and battle was soon joined. The fight was short and conclusive. Ariovistus was chased back across the Rhine and apparently died soon afterwards.

Julius Caesar had accomplished all this in the one campaigning season of the summer of 58. He had advanced his army a long way north into Gaul—all in the interest of helping Rome's friends—and it now became clear that he intended to stay. From this time on Caesar seems to have felt that he had every right to be where he was, and that all of Gaul now owed Rome some loyalty. In the following winter he did not withdraw his army to the Province, but left it in northern Gaul, while he went to the extreme southernmost part of the Province—North Italy. Here he could be in touch with affairs in Rome, while remaining within the boundary of his province, which he was not allowed to leave. This was to be the pattern for most of the years that Caesar was in Gaul.

The summer of 57 saw Caesar's penetration of Gaul completed. Many Gauls must have already been regretting that Caesar had ever been invited in, and the Belgae, the group of tribes who occupied Belgium and Holland, prepared for war. This brought Caesar and his army down among them, while he sent his lieutenant Publius Crassus, the son of his ally, to crush the Veneti, a seafaring people who lived in Brittany. The Belgae were soon defeated or converted into "friends", but the campaign against the Veneti took two years. The Veneti were better seamen than the Romans, who were not used to the tides of the Atlantic. The Veneti used heavy, flat-bottomed sailing vessels that could not be harmed by the lighter Roman craft and were only defeated when the Romans invented a device for cutting loose their sails. When the Veneti surrendered, they were massacred or sold as slaves. Julius Caesar usually took care to seem a kind, reasonable man, but he could be merciless against anyone who caused him much trouble.

By 55 Caesar's hold on Gaul seemed to be complete. Early in that year he led an expedition against two Germanic tribes which crossed the Rhine into Gaul, chasing them back and leading a brief raid into Germany itself. All this took until the middle of August, when he set off on the first of his two celebrated expeditions to Britain.

The fact that Julius Caesar felt safe enough to leave Gaul behind him and go to Britain, which was then almost unknown to Rome, shows that he was quite confident about the Gallic situation. In one sense, he had good reason to be. In the course of four years he had trained and enlarged his army, and had also trained good officers. Also the Gauls were pacified, or at least quiet. Even so, it hardly seems that the expedition was quite worth the effort. Caesar himself says, in his book *On the Gallic War*, that the Britons, people closely allied to the mainland Gauls in race and language, had been giving aid to his enemies. By that time, however, he controlled the English channel, so the Britons cannot have been a serious threat. Probably he was chiefly interested in the glory of being the first Roman general to reach Britain.

*Plan of a battle, with the Romans attacking a Gallic camp.* ▷

# THE TRIBES OF BRITAIN

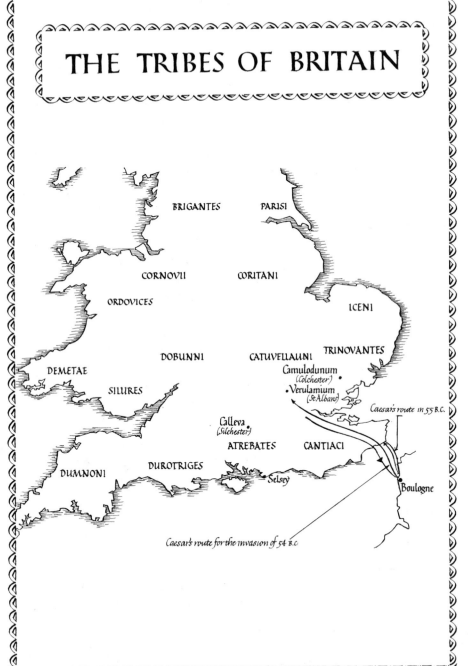

BRIGANTES

PARISI

CORNOVII

CORITANI

ORDOVICES

ICENI

DOBUNNI

CATUVELLAUNI

TRINOVANTES

DEMETAE

Camulodunum
(Colchester)

SILURES

Verulamium
(St.Albans)

Caesar's route in 55 B.C.

Calleva
(Silchester)

ATREBATES

CANTIACI

DUMNONI

DUROTRIGES

Selsey

Boulogne

Caesar's route for the invasion of 54 B.C.

Caesar led expeditions against Britain in 55 and again in 54. The first was quite a small demonstration against the tribes of the south coast. He stayed only a few days, did not advance far from the beach, and was for a time in serious danger by a storm that wrecked his fleet after he had left it riding at anchor on an open beach, without even the protection of a natural harbour, and quite at the mercy of bad weather.

The expedition of 54 was on a larger scale, and accomplished a little more. Again he landed on the coast of Kent, but this time he was able to march north, cross the Thames against stiff opposition, and win a battle against the powerful King Cassivellaunus somewhere in Essex. On this expedition he was also able to win allies in Britain, chiefly among the enemies of Cassivellaunus. This king, forced to make some kind of submission, promised to send tribute. However, Caesar soon returned to the continent with all his men and almost certainly no tribute was ever paid. Probably Caesar did not care very much.

In some ways his visits to Britain are puzzling. For one thing, Caesar seems to have shown less than his usual foresight, as he allowed his fleet to be damaged in 54 by just such a storm as had wrecked it in 55. Also, it was clear, even before he left the continent the second time, that many Gallic tribes were becoming restless. He was even forced to march against the Treveri of North-east Gaul, because they were plotting with the Germans, and when he left for Britain he took numerous Gallic leaders with him as hostages. When he returned, he found that a serious revolt was brewing, and it was not really until the end of 51 that this disturbance was completely crushed.

Considering how careful a planner Caesar was, it almost seems that he deliberately allowed his grip on Gaul to slacken a little in 54. If his work there had been too obviously completed by then, he might possibly have been recalled to Rome at an inconvenient time. This cannot be proved, but either Caesar was very carefully planning his ten years in Gaul, or he was very lucky with the timing of the war. As it happened, his troops had the whole of 50 in which to rest, and perhaps to become bored and ready for more adventures, before Caesar led them home in civil war in 49. He had long known that when his command expired in this year, he might be forced to revert to the status of a private citizen, if only for a short time. He would thus be exposed to prosecution and, rather than allow this to happen, he was prepared to begin a civil war. Caesar's plans were laid well in advance and, when the time came, his soldiers were ready.

We need not go into the details of the great Gallic revolt. Its leader was the brilliant but tragic prince Vercingetorix. This man was a fine general who understood that the best way to defeat Caesar was through guerilla tactics, and the policy which we call "scorched earth". Partly by accident, partly by the too-great enthusiasm of his followers, Vercingetorix was trapped in the siege of a town that he had not wanted to defend, and in 52 he surrendered to Caesar. He was kept as a prisoner for six years, and then killed. With him went Gaul's last real hope of freedom.

The story of Caesar's campaigns in Gaul is an interesting and exciting one which deserves far more space than it can be given here. It is a story of Caesar now marching across Gaul with a small party, desperately trying to catch up with his hard-pressed army; now trying to relieve a Roman legion besieged by Gauls, while a message telling that help was coming stuck unnoticed on a wall in the defenders' camp for several days, attached to a javelin. It is also the story of the conquest of a free people by an enemy cleverer and more unscrupulous than they. Anyone who wants to know more can do no better than read Caesar's own account. Since the time it was written, Caesar's book *On the Gallic War* has been recognised as the most brilliantly direct account of its kind ever written. He composed it as an outline for anyone who might want to write a full-dress history, but in its own way it is perfect, and no-one has ever tried to improve it.

A whole book could be written about Julius Caesar's talents as a

*A "triumph" in Rome—it was after being displayed on such an occasion that the unlucky Vercingetorix was executed.*

*(overleaf) The Roman lighthouse at Dover, remnant of the 400 years of Roman occupation of Britain.*

soldier. He seems to have owed his great success to three things: speed and capacity for hard work, an ability to make fast decisions and take advantage of his luck, and a wonderful power to make his troops love him. He was able to enforce stern discipline when this was necessary, but he did not object to his men running riot at other times. "My men fight just as well when they stink of perfume", he is supposed to have said. Once he was on a journey, away from his army, accompanied only by an old and sickly officer. At night they found a shelter roomy enough for only one man, and Caesar slept in the open.

When he sent messengers to announce the arrival of his army, Suetonius says, he would often appear ahead of the messengers. Though not a young man, he would expose himself to hardships as great as the army suffered. Nor did he ignore the private soldier. Julius Caesar's books on his campaigns are full of references to humble soldiers who did brave things. Caesar took a personal interest in every man in his army. They loved him for it, and fought all the harder.

# MEANWHILE AT ROME

One of the secrets of Julius Caesar's success lies in the way he was able to act decisively in many concerns at the same time. While he was fighting a very long and sometimes difficult campaign in Gaul, he also managed to keep going his interests in Rome. This he did partly through the many supporters that he had been careful to recruit. They continually wrote him letters about the situation in Rome. In return, he gave them orders and they distributed his propaganda.

Troubles began for him at Rome almost as soon as he had left. Very soon, Crassus and particularly Pompey began to suspect that they had raised up in Caesar a man who would be more than a match for them, and Caesar's enemies began working assiduously to detach Pompey from him. Pompey was particularly annoyed by a young popular agitator named Clodius, who recruited a band of thugs, and made Pompey's life such a misery that he was barely able to leave his house. This was especially aggravating to Pompey since he was a man of few ideas, who cared only to appear in public surrounded by a flock of admirers. When forced to stay out of sight, he felt powerless and humiliated. Clodius had previously worked for Caesar, and so Pompey suspected the worst.

In fact, Caesar may not have been behind Clodius' activities, since Clodius was a very independent-minded, unstable man. Quite possibly he was playing his own game at this time. Pompey's response to Clodius was to have a friend recruit a rival gang, which confronted Clodius' men and plunged Rome into gang warfare which

lasted unchecked for a number of years. Finally, in 52, Pompey's gang succeeded in killing Clodius.

Another source of irritation was the King of Egypt. This man, a weak ruler who was totally dependent on Roman support, had been ejected by his subjects in 58, and was in Rome asking for help in being restored. Both Pompey and Crassus wanted to lead the Senatorial commission which would take him back to Egypt. This became a powerful source of rivalry in their coalition.

By early 56, the alliance of Caesar, Pompey, and Crassus was thus in great danger of collapsing. To make matters worse, the conservative Lucius Domitius Ahenobarbus, who was a candidate for the Consulship in 55, announced that, if elected, he would recall Caesar from Gaul. Faced with this crisis, Caesar worked hard to arrange a conference with his two allies, where he would try to keep their coalition alive. The three men finally met in Luca, a town in North Italy just inside Caesar's province, which as governor he was not allowed to leave before his office expired. The majority of Rome's senators now felt themselves to be dependent on one or other of the the three men, and many senators travelled to Luca to wait on their masters—a sign of how far the republic had decayed.

At this conference the three men decided that they could still work together, and they planned the way in which they would continue to dominate the state for their mutual advantage. They would force the election of Pompey and Crassus as Consuls for 55, thus circumventing the danger to Caesar. After their term in office, both Pompey and Crassus would receive important commands to match Caesar's growing prestige. Pompey took Spain. He had no interest in fighting there and, in fact, stayed for the next few years near Rome, governing the province through subordinates. Crassus was bolder. Though now over sixty years old, he foolishly wanted to gain a military reputation, and so he was made Governor of Syria, where there was the prospect of a war against the powerful empire of Parthia.

◁ *Ptolemy XII.*

Caesar was given another five years in Gaul, his term to expire in 49, and the King of Egypt was restored by Gabinus, a man of lesser stature who might not use the occasion to aggrandise himself and who was thus acceptable as a compromise to all three confederates.

We can probably see Caesar's brain behind these compromises; but in any case the new arrangement did not last very long. In 54, Julia, who was Caesar's daughter and had been married to Pompey as part of the deal of 60, died. The marriage had been one of political convenience, but it is certain that Pompey and Julia were genuinely fond of each other. Julia must often have been useful in smoothing out differences between her husband and father. Her death thus removed an important link between them. When Pompey remarried, it was not to a relative of Caesar, as Caesar had hoped, but to a lady from the opposing faction.

The other great blow to the confederacy was Crassus' death. As a younger man, he had achieved some fame as a commander of soldiers, but it would have taken a much better man than the elderly Crassus to conquer the Parthians. These people ruled a large empire around present-day Iran and extended almost to the shore of the Mediterranean. They were expert at fighting from horseback, and their favourite tactic was to lure an enemy ever deeper into their country by pretending to run away, and then suddenly turn and attack when the invader had become too confident. The Parthians were the only foreign power that Rome was obliged to treat as an equal. Realistically, Rome could never hope to do more than come to a face-saving agreement with Parthia, and to leave that country in peace. The Parthians dealt with Crassus in the same way as the rest of their enemies. They lured his army into a desert, and then attacked, destroying it almost to the last man. Crassus himself was killed.

From this time on, relations between Pompey and Caesar deteriorated steadily. United with Crassus, and each of the three using his loyal supporters, they had so completely gained control of the elections and appointments at Rome, that in a sense the free republic was already

*A Statuette of a Parthian horseman.*

dead. It was now only a matter of time before they would be fighting each other, and the republic's demise would then be plain to all. For a while, however, they still preserved the outward appearance of an alliance. The rioting previously mentioned was still going on, and it reached a point where Pompey was for a short time given by the Senate the extraordinary position of "Sole Consul" to combat it. Caesar objected that this violated the spirit of their agreement that one of them should not gain more prestige or authority than the other. Pompey appeared to agree and, to compensate Caesar, he arranged, through his influence and connections, for a special law to be passed to allow Caesar to stand for the Consulship without actually coming to Rome. Caesar had hoped for something like that. He had always known that, in order to stand for a second Consulship, he would have to leave the army, and come to Rome as a private citizen (when he could of course be prosecuted for the irregularities of his first Consulship, and so blocked from being elected again). Thus, in theory at least, his constitutional problem was solved. However, this new law existed only through Pompey's good will. It could easily be rescinded and, in fact, Caesar never had a chance to invoke it. This law was the last thing that Pompey ever did for Caesar. By 52, increasingly drawn to the conservatives, he was more and more openly Caesar's enemy.

So matters dragged on into 50, with Caesar's campaign in Gaul virtually over, and people increasingly worried about what would happen when his term of office expired there in 49. The alternative of another Consulship for Julius Caesar, or Julius Caesar leading his army against Rome, seemed clear. The majority of Senators wanted to avoid a crisis and give Caesar his Consulship, but a small group of extreme conservatives, led by Cato, were determined to force the issue. Throughout 50, this group tried to make the Senate discuss the matter of recalling Caesar, now that Gaul was quiet. Caesar's friends in the Senate always managed to prevent this discussion. But a crisis was approaching, and civil war was in the air. By now

Pompey had also been voted troops—ostensibly for other purposes, but troops which he could well use to fight Caesar. On December 1, 50 BC the Tribune of the People Gaius Scribonius Curio, a follower of Caesar, forced the Senate to vote on a proposal that both Pompey and Caesar should disarm. So great was the desire for peace that all but a tiny minority of the Senate supported this measure, but it too was vetoed by a Tribune from the extreme conservative group.

Events now moved very fast. On the next day, the Consul asked Pompey to save the state by taking command of all troops in Italy. This he did, thus finally committing himself to civil war. Caesar was now moving his army down the Italian peninsula, but not yet out of his province. The surviving sources show that, even at this late time, Caesar was negotiating very hard to prevent war. He corresponded with the Senate, and also with Pompey privately, but to no avail.

On January 7, 49 BC, the crisis came. Curio (who had just left office as a Tribune of the People) and Marcus Antonius—known to history as Mark Antony (one of Caesar's supporters among the Tribunes for 49) — were warned to leave Rome for their own safety. By night they fled in disguise to Caesar. Julius Caesar took this as a declaration of war.

As long as Caesar kept his army within his province, he was committing no crime, but to march it into Italy proper without leave was an act of civil war. Plutarch tells what happened, and his account is probably true, as he takes it from the writings of the historian Asinius Pollio, who was there.

"Caesar spent the day in public, standing about and watching gladiators perform. A little before dinner he bathed, dressed, and went to the banqueting hall, where he chatted briefly with those who had been invited to dinner. When it was almost dark he stood up and left, apologising to most of the guests, and saying that he would soon be back. But a few of his friends he had previously instructed to follow him, not in a body, but by

*An impression of Caesar crossing the River Rubicon.*

various different routes.

"When he came to the river which separated his province from Italy proper (it is called the Rubicon), he began to consider what a huge and terrible thing he was about to do, and slowed down.

"For a long time he talked indecisively with the friends that were with him, including Asinius Pollio. Finally however, in a kind of emotional outburst, he seemed to abandon thought and make a leap at the future, saying, as men often do when they begin some desperate and unpredictable undertaking; 'Let's throw the dice!' With this he hastened across the river."

*A gladiator.*

# DICTATOR

When Julius Caesar marched his army into Italy, he was probably expecting severe resistance before he could reach Rome. This did not happen. For some reason Pompey, who of course commanded all the troops against Caesar, decided not to fight in Italy, but to evacuate his forces to Greece and make a stand there. There may have been some good strategic reasons for this, but psychologically it was disastrous. Most of his supporters—whom we can now call republicans—felt that Pompey had no heart for the war. It seemed as if he thought he was defeated from the very beginning, and of course this attitude infected his men.

While Pompey and his army were on their way to Greece, Caesar arrived in Rome, where he addressed such Senators as had not fled, and tried to defend his actions. He also broke into the public treasury and helped himself to all the money that he and his army needed. From this time on, Caesar was really in control of things at Rome. The story of his battles with the republican forces is a complicated one, and for this book a brief summary will have to do. From 49 to 45 BC Caesar spent a great amount of time out of Rome, fighting Pompeian forces in Greece, Egypt, Africa and Spain. Pompey himself was soon removed from the scene. In 49 and early 48 he organised a clever defence against Caesar in Greece, and for a time almost looked like overcoming him. But in 48 Caesar was able to defeat Pompey at a place called Pharsalus. Pompey's army broke up and Pompey himself fled to Egypt, where the king, in panic at the prospect of Caesar arriving soon after, had him killed.

*The Roman Forum today*

Caesar claimed to regret this murder, and probably did, because he had been ostentatiously "pardoning" all republicans that came in his way, and no doubt he would have liked to show his clemency by pardoning Pompey as well. Caesar's own arrival in Egypt caused the murder of the king, and he was for several months involved in a bitter and complicated palace revolution there, from which he emerged as the champion of the queen, named Cleopatra, whom he set up as a ruler in her own right. With Pompey dead, it was necessary for Caesar only to overcome the remnants of his supporters, but this took him to every corner of the Roman empire and it was not until 45 that the last vestige of opposition had been defeated. By this time, all Caesar's opponents were converted into at least nominal friends, or killed. Cato, in particular, refused any pardon and, when he saw that his military position was hopeless, finally committed suicide in North Africa. Marcus Junius Brutus had been another of Caesar's enemies—not evidently on personal so much as on constitutional grounds—but Caesar took great pains to win him over after Pharsalus, much as Sulla had long ago wanted to bring the young Caesar to his own way of thinking. But Brutus lived to murder his benefactor.

Between 49 and 45, Julius Caesar was only in Rome for a total of a very few months, but in this time he accomplished a vast amount of reform. Once again we can see the strange combination of self-serving politician and wise statesman which was an important part of Caesar's nature. He attempted no less than a general reform of Roman life. As part of this programme, he initiated measures that were designed to reduce the excessive luxury that had been growing in recent years. These involved such diverse matters as the kind of material that could be used for women's dresses, and the number of courses that could be served at dinner. As can be imagined, these measures had only a very temporary success.

Caesar also attacked the problem of unemployment at Rome. This he did by organising a number of colonies of Roman citizens, to be founded outside Italy. Land was cheaper in the provinces, and there

*Statue of Brutus.*  ▷

*(above) Coin of Cleopatra and (right) remains in the Forum of the Temple dedicated by Julius Caesar to Venus Genetrix (the Mother) since he claimed descent from her. Beside her statue he placed one of Cleopatra.*

would be good opportunities for the colonists to support themselves. In this way the state would be relieved of a serious and politically dangerous burden and, as an additional benefit, Roman customs would be spread throughout the Mediterranean world. Caesar also worked to get Roman citizens back on to the land in Italy. Rich men were still holding far too much farmland there, and Caesar did little to take it away from them. However, he restricted the number of slaves that could be used on a farm, thus encouraging the hiring of free workers.

He was interested, as well, in giving people from the provinces more influence in the affairs of Rome. Their complete exclusion had been a serious grievance in the past, and something which had helped weaken the empire. Caesar worked to alleviate this problem, by admitting to the Senate men from outside Italy, probably Roman citizens whose ancestors had settled abroad, and by granting Roman citizenship to many deserving individuals. His successors continued this process, until finally the Roman empire was not a rule of Romans over provincials, but a state in which all men were Roman citizens. In future years, some of the best emperors came from outside Italy.

One of Caesar's most enduring reforms was a reorganisation of the calendar. Till this time, the Roman calendar had been a clumsy arrangement, where the year was only 355 days long, and an extra month was added every few years to keep the calendar in line with the seasons. Since the priests in charge of the calendar were also politicians, they had frequently interfered with the sequence of months for their own purposes. This of course created a great muddle, and by Caesar's time the calendar was about three months out of step with the seasons. Taking the advice of a Greek astronomer, he introduced a calendar of twelve months and 365 days. This is called the Julian Calendar and is almost exactly the same as the one used today. The seventh month was—and still is—named in his honour.

So much for his good actions. To appreciate why Julius Caesar was eventually murdered, it will be helpful to look at his constitutional position. From early 49, he completely dominated Rome, but, with

# THE JULIAN CALENDAR

Pre 46 B.C.    The added ten days → 46 B.C.

| | | |
|---:|:---:|:---|
| 29 | Januarius | 31 |
| 28 | Februarius | 28 |
| 31 | Martius | 31 |
| 29 | Aprilis | 30 |
| 31 | Maius | 31 |
| 29 | Junius | 30 |
| 31 | Quintilis (Julius) | 31 |
| 29 | Sextilis | 31 |
| 31 | September | 30 |
| 29 | October | 31 |
| 29 | Novembris | 30 |
| 29 | December | 31 |
| ___ | | ___ |
| 355 | | 365 |

1st January to 21st March counted
as beginning of the year.

1st January fixed as
beginning of the year.
February has 29 days every 4th year.

a truly Roman interest in titles and offices, he was careful to take some legal-seeming grant of power. At times he was elected to the Consulship—with no opposition, of course. At times he abandoned the Consulship in favour of a higher office, that of Dictator. The Dictator was an official who had been occasionally appointed in earlier years, usually when a great military crisis threatened. At such times it was not advisable to have two Consuls, who might disagree, at the head of the state. The Dictator was absolute ruler, but his term of office was only six months. Late in 46 BC Caesar laid down the Consulship for the last time, and took the Dictatorship for a period of ten years. Early in 44, he was given the Dictatorship for life.

Perpetual Dictatorship was, to the Romans, a complete contradiction in terms, and it must have seemed to many to be only another word for the hated title of "king". It was this which more than anything else caused Caesar's assassination, but in the last years of his life he did many other things that made him hated by those not of his party. He brought the notorious Cleopatra to Rome for a long visit, for instance, and this caused offence. The offence was all the greater in that she had given birth to a son whose father was probably Caesar himself. To make matters even worse, Cleopatra named the child "Caesarion". Caesar was growing old, and perhaps a little careless. Many republicans might have submitted to his rule, if he had not so often paraded its dictatorial aspect before them. On December 31, 45 BC, a Consul died, just a few hours before his term of office was to expire. A friend of Caesar asked to be given the Consulship for what was left of the day, and Caesar agreed. This mockery of republican institutions was something which many people could not endure. Cicero said of Caesar's appointee, with bitter humour, that he was a very fine Consul since he had never slept throughout his term of office.

Another problem was that Caesar did not have much spare time for conciliating his old enemies. Cicero, for instance, had been a half-hearted partisan of Pompey, but quickly made his peace with Caesar.

*Cleopatra presenting her son Caesarion to the Gods of Egypt.*

Shortly before Caesar's death, Cicero went to visit him. He was kept waiting. Caesar noticed this, and said, "Am I foolish enough to think that this man is my friend, easygoing as he is, when he has to sit for so long and wait for my convenience?" Cicero records this remark in a letter.

Above all, there was the question of Caesar's ultimate plans for Rome. We do not know what these were, as he died before he could carry them out, but there is a strong possibility that he wanted to revive the kingship. At this time he took to wearing high red boots, which were to the Romans a sign of royalty, and long ago he had stressed his family's connection with the old kings of Rome. Rumours about this flew everywhere, and it was in this atmosphere that a conspiracy formed to kill him.

*Coin of Caesar the "Perpetual Dictator".*

# ASSASSINATION

Caesar the revolutionary was bad enough, but to many people Caesar the potential king could be dealt with only by assassination. Early in 45 about sixty men formed a conspiracy with the intention of killing the dictator and restoring liberty.

The conspirators had good reason to be alarmed. Caesar had begun acting like a king, in the ways already mentioned, and there was evidence that he would soon have the title as well as the substance. Rumours abounded. It was said that he would transfer the empire's capital to Alexandria (out of love for Cleopatra) or elsewhere. He planned soon to lead an army against the Parthians, and an oracle was in circulation at this time, to the effect that the Parthians could be conquered only by a king.

He was even offered a crown. Early in 44, Caesar was presiding at a religious festival. This was a celebration known as the Lupercalia, or Festival of Wolf-Running. In it, men ran a foot-race, dressed only in wolf-skins. One of the participants was Mark Antony, then a Consul. At the end of the race, he came up to Caesar's chair and offered him a diadem, the symbol of royalty.

Caesar was already dressed in a garb reminiscent of the ancient Roman kings but, when Antony placed the diadem on his head, he removed it. Most of the bystanders applauded this, taking it as a sign that he did not want to be king. What was meant by this demonstration is not clear. Antony, a friend and confederate of Caesar, would hardly have done it without mentioning it to the dictator first. Many of Caesar's enemies felt that the whole episode

*Statuette of the wolf suckling Romulus and Remus, the founders of Rome.*

was a test of public opinion. If the onlookers had cheered, they said, Caesar would have proclaimed himself king then and there. This is quite possible, but we cannot know for certain.

It is clear that Caesar's popularity with the people, on which he had always leaned heavily, was lessening. Recently he had been doing things on his own initiative that should have been done by vote of the people. The people of course knew that they were now ruled by a quasi-monarch, but still they resented any interference with the vote. Caesar had gone out of his way to conciliate the people by sponsoring elaborate public dinners at his own expense, but this was not altogether successful.

So the conspirators felt that their time was coming. On March 15, 44 BC, Julius Caesar was planning to make a speech to the Senate. Afterwards he would be leaving with his army to attack Parthia. From this time on, surrounded by his loyal troops, he would be relatively inaccessible to murder. Also, it seemed possible that he might be made king at that meeting of the Senate. Hence March 15 was at once the last chance to kill Caesar, and a good moment for asserting the freedom of the republic. It is not certain whether he really would have been made king at that time. Some sources say that Caesar would have been offered the kingship, to take effect only outside Italy. This may be true, or it may only reflect the propaganda of his enemies. Plutarch says that Caesar almost decided not to go to the Senate, because of bad omens and his wife's uneasiness, but the conspirators reassured him, saying that the Senate would vote him the kingship that day. Suetonius does not mention the conspirators tempting Caesar with the kingship, but only says that Caesar was discouraged by his wife's misgivings, and the fact that he was not feeling well that morning. His account is simpler than Plutarch's and is probably nearer the truth.

As far as we can tell, the conspirators acted from quite selfless motives. The leaders were all either men who had served with Caesar for many years, or men who had fought for Pompey, been pardoned and then entrusted with important jobs in government. The famous Brutus, whose full name was Marcus Junius Brutus, had for years been an outspoken republican and well respected as a man of great integrity; after Pharsalus Caesar was very careful that no harm come to him. Brutus was reconciled to Caesar and served for a time as a provincial governor. Cassius was another republican, pardoned after Pharsalus, who had been honoured by Caesar. Gaius Trebonius had served Caesar as a political agent—in fact, organising the law of 55 BC which gave Pompey and Crassus their provincial commands. Decimus Junius Brutus, a distant cousin of the other Brutus, had served with Caesar in Gaul and would have been Consul, by Caesar's wish, in 42.

All these conspirators renounced whatever future they might have had under Caesar's rule and decided that, for the good of Rome, he must die. Marcus Brutus, however, was their figurehead, and Plutarch says that none of the conspirators would move until Brutus joined them. There were two reasons for this. Not only was Brutus a man so well respected that nobody would suspect him with an evil motive in killing Caesar, but also he was well qualified for the task from the accident of his birth. He claimed to be descended from another Marcus Brutus, who was one of Rome's national heroes. In 509 BC this man had ejected the last king of Rome, and been instrumental in setting up the republic. Brutus was thus the obvious man to kill Caesar. It should be noted, however, that while by Roman standards he was a philosopher and a very upright man, his goodness was somewhat patchy. It had not prevented him, a few years previously, from lending money to a town in Cyprus at the unbelievable rate of 48% compound interest. This loan was probably illegal under Roman law, and there was no justification at all for the violent methods which Brutus' agents used to collect the debt.

In the months before the assassination, Caesar's enemies worked on Brutus, persuading him to join the conspiracy. On the walls of his house, and on his chair of office, there appeared such slogans as

"Brutus, are you asleep?"; "You are no true Brutus"; and "We need a Brutus today."

Caesar's enemies also tried to force matters along by speaking publicly of giving Caesar royal honours. Probably some of the current stories about Caesar wanting to be king originated from their propaganda. On one occasion at least it is fairly certain that this is what happened. One day Caesar's statue, set in the place where the Romans gathered to listen to speeches, was found crowned with a diadem. Two tribunes of the people immediately removed it. Caesar was greatly displeased. He may not have wanted the diadem at that point, but he seems to have felt that its removal was a personal insult, or an attempt to undermine his dignity. He complained to the Senate and had the two tribunes removed from office. If this was an attempt by his enemies to embarrass him, it succeeded very well.

So the conspiracy developed. Julius Caesar probably did not know of it in detail, but he was well aware that his enemies might be plotting. In all probability—and this is greatly to his credit—he did not care too much. For some years he had been escorted by a bodyguard of Spanish soldiers, but not long before his death, he had dismissed them. He is supposed to have said something to the effect that a life surrounded by guards is not worth living. Suetonius says that the only measures he took against the various conspiracies that he discovered was to announce in public that he knew about them. Caesar was getting old, and possibly he did not want to live into extreme old age. Always a believer in luck—of which he had had plenty up to that time—he probably felt that he could rely on his luck in this matter as well and, if not, it mattered little. Both Suetonius and Plutarch recount that, at dinner on the evening before he was killed, someone asked him what sort of death he would prefer, and he replied, "A sudden one".

Any English-speaking person who reads the story of Julius Caesar's death will probably have another account in mind—the one given in Shakespeare's play *Julius Caesar*. This play is, of course, not a

79

primary source on Caesar's life, as Shakespeare had no more information than any writer of the present day. It is, however, a very faithful dramatic rendering of the circumstances of Caesar's death, and the motives which he gives to the various characters are quite credible. Shakespeare draws his material almost entirely from Plutarch, who was then much better known than many of the other ancient sources of this period. He makes extensive use of Plutarch's lives of Caesar, Brutus, Antony, and Cato. The speeches are often adaptations of things said by Plutarch, and it is quite possible to read the play along with Plutarch's *Lives*, picking out the source for different episodes in the play. Shakespeare's *Julius Caesar* is drama, not history, but it is a very faithful dramatization of good historical sources.

So Julius Caesar was manoeuvred to his death. He was killed by men whom he trusted, but at the end of a life that had been dedicated to revolutionizing Rome. It was at least fitting, if not planned, that he fell at the foot of Pompey's statue, thus seeming to be a sacrifice to the old republic which he had destroyed.

*Coin of Brutus celebrating the assassination on the Ides of March.*

# AFTERMATH

And so the murder was done. Caesar was dead. But the conspirators were soon to discover that getting Caesar out of the way was not going to solve the multitude of problems that beset the republic. The forces of history are not easy to stop, and the republic was dead as surely as Caesar, who had given it its death blow. What followed the assassination was a period of chaos, perhaps grimmer than even that which came with the drive for power of Marius and Sulla.

Rome was without a leader. On everyone's mind was the question "Who would take charge?" But first Caesar had to be buried. In the general shock immediately after the murder, the people of Rome, who had not been so fond of Caesar recently as earlier, could evidently have been persuaded to side either with or against the murderers. However, Antony took the initiative. He made an inflammatory speech, showed the Dictator's mangled body to the crowds and aroused their feelings. He also read Caesar's will aloud to them. When the mob heard that Caesar had left a sum of money to each citizen, as well as some gardens that were to be made into a public park, their feelings turned to hatred of the murderers. The crowd seized his body and, taking benches from the Senate chamber for firewood, they cremated him, then and there, in Rome's chief market-place. Although the mob's attempt to burn down the houses of the conspirators was unsuccessful it was clear to the murderers that they must leave Rome at once.

The last hope of restoring the republic had now gone. The conspirators had hoped that, with Caesar dead, the Senate would at once

*View of the Forum today, showing the Rostra, left centre (between the three columns and the Arch), from which Mark Antony delivered Caesar's funeral oration.*

assert its old authority, but, after many years of domination by powerful individuals, the Senate's instinct was now not to give orders, but to obey. They would easily bow to the will of any strong man, and such a person was Mark Antony.

The conspirators' greatest mistake had been not to kill Antony along with his master. Scruples had prevented this: Brutus had felt that Caesar alone was the cause of the mischief and insisted that Caesar alone should die. Antony was still Consul, and he was more than ready to carry Rome down the path of dictatorship that Caesar had so clearly marked out. However, he had overlooked a small detail—small but ultimately fatal to him. In his will Caesar had left the better part of his estate to his grand-nephew Octavian. He also posthumously adopted this man as his son. We have no way of knowing if this meant that Caesar felt that Octavian was the man to succeed him, any more than we know anything else about his final plans. As it turned out, Octavian was a very worthy heir and, after a terrible civil war, managed to take over his adoptive father's place.

*Coins of Mark Antony and Lepidus who together with Octavius formed a Triumvirate, overcame Brutus and Cassius at Philippi and ruled Rome for a time.*

Octavian was in Greece when he learned of the assassination and, copying Caesar when he heard of Sulla's death, he set out for Rome to seek his fortune. There he found Antony hostile, and inclined to dismiss him; he was, after all, not yet twenty years old. Relying on Caesar's name, Octavian raised a private army and forced Antony to recognize him as an equal. For some years, the two maintained an uneasy partnership, but inevitably their jealousies at last erupted in civil war, the most grievous the country had yet seen. This ended in 32 BC with Octavian dominating the state, and his enemies dead. He held power until his death in AD 14 , and finished the work that Caesar had started.

In one regard Octavian learned from Caesar's mistake. He was very careful to avoid anything that might suggest kingship. Instead he very carefully put up a facade of maintaining a free government, with himself as a regularly elected official. Unlike Caesar, he showed great tact in not giving offence. We even possess an official document

*Coin of Octavian.*

*Statue of Octavian as Augustus Caesar.* ▷

84

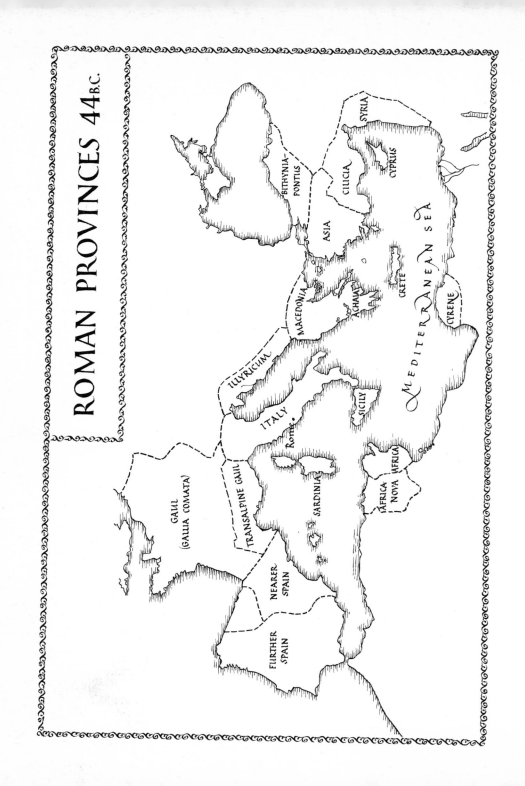

ROMAN PROVINCES 44 B.C.

from the period in which he said "I restored the republic." Of course this was not true and fooled no-one; people knew he held absolute power, but this pretence eased the way and made his enlightened despotism more acceptable. Although not king in name, in fact he held more power than any of the old kings of Rome. He was even able to name his successor, and in reality he was the first Roman emperor. After him, there were emperors in Rome for more than 400 years. To mark his new position, the Senate gave him the imperial-sounding name or title "Augustus", and it is by this name that history remembers him.

It is probably true that when Augustus took over, it was the state's only way of ending the futile civil wars. Augustus' rule started a period known as the *Pax Romana*, or "Roman peace", when for the only time in its history Rome was more or less free from the nagging wars with which it was usually involved. Augustus set the pattern for one-man rule which was followed until the final collapse of the empire.

However, if Augustus finally reorganized the Roman Empire, his success was only due to Caesar's first effort in that direction. Caesar was the only man of his generation who had the ability and the will to make himself ruler of Rome. Certainly Pompey could never have done it. Moreover, Augustus could not have taken over, if he had not been Caesar's heir. Also, he could probably not have maintained his long, peaceful rule without the example of Julius Caesar's murder behind him. Caesar's death, and the turmoil that followed it, so horrified the Romans that they were happy to be quietly ruled by Augustus, even if they had to lose some freedom.

The conclusion is that, without Julius Caesar's life and death, the Roman Empire would most probably not have survived very long. The effects of this would have been enormous, and the whole course of world history would have been very different. It is no exaggeration to say that the world as we know it, for good or ill, is as it is because of Julius Caesar.

Julius Caesar

Augustus

Tiberius

Caligula

Claudius

Nero

Galba

Otho

Vitellius

Vespasian

Titus

Domitian

*Coins of the Twelve Caesars.*

# APPENDIX I
# ROMAN NAMES

In very earliest times, a Roman would have had two names; a personal name, and a name which belonged to his family. Thus he might be called Marcus Junius, or Lucius Tarquinius, in the way that a modern man is called John Smith or James Brown. The Latin terms for the personal name and family name are, respectively, *Praenomen* and *Nomen*.

Roman families tended to stick together, and it would not be many generations before a family that had started out with one couple had produced a large network of cousins and collaterals, who were bound together in a sizeable clan-like organization. The *nomen*, like Junius, would then be the name of the whole clan. As these clans developed, people within them often took a third name, to distinguish themselves from relatives who might have the same *praenomen* and *nomen*. This third name, called a *cognomen*, was placed after the *nomen*. It was often a kind of nickname—not always flattering—and the descendants of its first bearer usually kept it.

The *cognomen* might come from anything memorable about the man. Thus an early Marcus Junius took the *cognomen* Brutus, which means "stupid". An early Marcus Tullius took the name Cicero, which has to do with the Latin word *cicer*, or "chick-pea". This man had a bulbous nose which looked like a pea, and he passed the name down to his famous descendant, the orator and philosopher of Caesar's time.

Caesar's full name was Gaius Julius Caesar, and the word Caesar seems to mean "hairy". This is ironic, since our Caesar was somewhat bald.

In modern writings about Romans there are quite arbitrary conventions about which name is used to refer to each man, though if the individual is well known, it is more common to call him by his *cognomen*. There are, however, many exceptions to this. For instance, the historian Suetonius' full name was Gaius Suetonius Tranquillus, and we always refer to him by his *nomen*.

In the case of a few of the best-known figures, the name is made over into an English form. Thus Gnaeus Pompeius Magnus is known to the English-speaking world as "Pompey", and the conspirator Lucius Sergius Catilina as "Catiline".

Here are some full names of people mentioned in this book, with the name by which the man is usually known in italics. By Julius Caesar's time almost every Roman had three names. A very few had no *cognomen* and went by only the original two. The most famous example of this is Caesar's uncle, the general and politician Gaius Marius.

Marcus Calpurnius *Bibulus*
Marcus Junius *Brutus*
*Decimus* Junius *Brutus* Albinus
Gaius *Cassius* Longinus
Lucius Sergius Catilina, known as *Catiline*
Marcus Porcius *Cato*
Marcus Tullius *Cicero*
Lucius Cornelius *Cinna*
Publius *Clodius* Pulcher
Marcus Licinius *Crassus*
Gaius Scribonius *Curio*
*Julia* (Caesar's aunt)
*Julia* (Caesar's daughter)
Gaius *Julius Caesar*
Lucius *Lucceius*
Marcus Antonius, known as *Mark Antony*

Gaius *Marius*
Gaius Julius Caesar Octavianus, known as *Octavian*, later called
   *Augustus*
Gnaeus Pompeius Magnus, known as *Pompey*
Lucius Cornelius *Sulla*
Gaius *Trebonius*
Publius *Vatinius*

# APPENDIX II
# SOURCES

## Ancient Sources

There is no one complete ancient account of Caesar's life, written near the time when the events occurred. The story can, however, be pieced together quite clearly from a variety of ancient writers, and the most important of these are listed below, in the order in which they lived.

*Caesar himself*. Caesar's books *On the Gallic War* and *On the Civil War* give a wonderfully clear account of these wars. He is, of course, biased in his own favour, but does not seem to tamper seriously with the truth. He wrote nothing that survives about the rest of his life.

*Cicero*. Marcus Tullius Cicero, the great Roman orator, politician and philosopher, was a very close contemporary of Caesar, and was killed in the civil wars that followed the dictator's death. Any treatment of Caesar more detailed than the present book would have a lot to say about Cicero, but Cicero's influence had greatly declined by the time Caesar rose to power, and nothing that he did was really crucial to Caesar's career. Many of his surviving speeches give a wealth of detail about the life and politics of the time. We also have a large collection of his private letters, which at times give an almost minute-by-minute account of events. Unfortunately, he wrote nothing about the actual murder of Julius Caesar.

*Suetonius*. Gaius Suetonius Tranquillus was a secretary to the Emperor Hadrian in the early second century AD. He wrote biographies of Julius Caesar and the eleven emperors who followed him. This work is usually known in English as *The Twelve Caesars*. Suetonius was a careful biographer, who was greatly interested in preserving interesting stories and gossip about his subjects. He understood the workings of the republic in its last century quite well, and he is particularly valuable in that he had access to imperial archives, where he found much useful material.

*Plutarch*. Unlike the previous writers, who wrote in Latin, Plutarch was a Greek, though a Roman citizen, and he wrote in his native language. He lived at the same time as Suetonius, and among many other works wrote a series of ''Parallel Lives''—paired biographies of a Greek and a Roman who had done similar things. While his intellect was clearly superior to that of Suetonius, he is sometimes less useful because he tends to let artistic and philosophical considerations interfere with the telling of a simple story. He is not quite as accurate as Suetonius, and has much less background knowledge of Roman affairs. Even so, his *Lives* of Caesar, Brutus, Pompey, Crassus, Cato, Cicero and Antony are very important for anyone studying this period.

*Cassius Dio*. Cassius Dio Cocceianus, also a Greek with Roman citizenship, wrote in Greek a history of Rome from earliest times down to his own day, the year AD 229. As with Suetonius and Plutarch, his account is detailed and careful, and draws on eye-witness evidence not available to us. However, he was living in a time when the Roman empire was fast becoming an absolute despotism, and his understanding of the workings of a free republic is even more defective than Plutarch's. He is very useful in filling in gaps left by other writers.

For anyone who wants to read about this period from the ancient sources, there are good *Penguin* translations of Caesar, Suetonius, Plutarch and parts of Cicero. The works of any of the writers mentioned above could be found in a larger public library, together with much else from Greek and Roman antiquity.

### Modern Works

There are many modern writings, of varying quality, about the life and times of Julius Caesar. One of the best general histories of the period is *From the Gracchi to Nero*, by H. H. Scullard.

The best work on Caesar himself, at once scholarly and very readable, is *Caesar*, by Matthias Gelzer, translated from the German by Peter Needham.

A shorter book of the same type is *Julius Caesar*, by J. P. V. D. Balsdon.

The standard work on Roman life and customs, also very readable, is *Daily Life in Ancient Rome*, by Jerome Carcopino.

# TRIBUNES OF THE PEOPLE
## APPENDIX III

These officials deserve a special mention, as they were important to Caesar's career, but did not quite fit into the regular structure of Roman government. In much earlier times—the 400's and 300's BC—there was a great deal of tension between the Senate, which represented the old landowning families, and the rest of the Roman people. The Senate tried to rule Rome in its own interest, and the people felt that they were powerless against it. As a result of much conflict this office, also known as the Tribunate of the Plebians, was instituted. The Tribunes were elected by the people, and they sat in the Senate with the purpose of watching what went on and looking out for the common people's interests. Any Tribune had the special power of being able to stop anything that was being done, either a debate or the passing of a law, simply by standing up and vetoing it.

By about 200 BC the original conflict between the Senate and the rest of Rome had been resolved, but the Tribunes remained. From being protectors of the people, they now became politicians with the same ambitions as any others in the Senate. Their veto was a weapon that could be used in anyone's interest. In Caesar's time Tribunes of the People used the veto in a conservative cause as often as any other.

# INDEX